Wire-Wrapped and Beaded Jewelry

Wire-Wrapped and Beaded Jewelry

J. Devlin Barrick, editor

Carolyn Yohn McManus,
artist and consultant

Photographs by
Carolyn Yohn McManus

STACKPOLE
BOOKS

Published by
STACKPOLE BOOKS
5067 Ritter Road
Mechanicsburg, PA 17055
www.stackpolebooks.com

Printed in China

10 9 8 7 6 5 4 3 2 1

First edition

All designs by Carolyn Yohn McManus,
  except Twist-and-Wrap Bracelet by Danielle Wilson.

Cover design by Caroline M. Stover

Library of Congress Cataloging-in-Publication Data

Wire-wrapped and beaded jewelry / J. Devlin Barrick,
editor ; Carolyn Yohn McManus, artist and consultant ;
photographs by Carolyn Yohn McManus. — 1st ed.
     p. cm.
  ISBN-13: 978-0-8117-3607-7
  ISBN-10: 0-8117-3607-5
  1. Jewelry making. 2. Wire craft. 3. Beadwork. I. Barrick, J. Devlin. II. McManus, Carolyn Yohn.
  TT212.W595 2009
  745.594'2—dc22
                              2008049631

Contents

Part Two: Metal 83

Acknowledgments

First, my heartiest thanks go to Carolyn Yohn McManus, whose designs and expertise are at the heart of this book. In just a few short visits, she passed on knowledge that will give us all creative ideas to last a lifetime. And she gave up her mornings before work to do so—she is a noble woman, indeed!

Next, I would like to acknowledge Rachael Ebersole, whose youthful hands grace the pages before you. Third, thanks to Danielle M. Wilson, whose twist-and-wrap bracelet adds variety to this collection.

My mentors at Stackpole Books, Mark Allison and Judith Schnell, sent me on this journey in the first place, and they supported and encouraged me at every turn. How lucky I am to have them as colleagues and friends.

My family members, especially Matthew, took over many hours of child care so I could deliver this project as promised. Jonas and Alainna tolerated a distracted mommy much better than most adults would. Without them, what would I do?

J. D. B.

Introduction

The projects you'll find here are introduced roughly in order of difficulty, based on the number of steps each project requires for completion. At first glance, you might browse each chapter opener to see which designs you like the looks of most, then read through the instructions to see if they seem feasible based on your experience. If you are just beginning, completing the projects in order will help you learn basic techniques that reappear throughout Part One.

Part Two—on riveting and precious metal clay—stands out from the first part of the book in that these projects use wire wrapping and beading only minimally. If you find these pieces intriguing, go ahead and jump right in, and don't let the number of steps intimidate you. When you break them down, they are actually easy projects, with truly creative results.

One thing Carolyn taught me is not to fuss too much over what stones to use or what bead combinations to dream up. These pieces come together best with a touch of spontaneity and experimentation. By using craft wire, you will have little money invested in each piece, so just let your fingers go to work and see what happens.

Go at your own pace, treat these steps as mere guidelines, and let your imagination take you beyond the ideas presented in this book. Have fun!

J. D. B.

Part One

Wire Wrapping

Tools and Materials

Your most valuable three tools will be round-nose pliers, chain-nose pliers, and a flush cutter. Let an experienced jewelry maker help you choose them if you're new to the art. If you're not, you already have your favorites on hand. Have these nearby before you begin every project.

Sterling wire is softer than craft wire and can be substituted for craft wire anytime—it is considerably more expensive, however, so you might choose to use it sparingly, and with experience. We'll use 18-, 22-, and 24-gauge craft wire throughout the projects here, so plan to have those thicknesses on hand. Fourteen-gauge craft wire and copper wire make an appearance in a few pieces, but you can wait until you're ready to work on those projects to see if you really need them.

If you want to just get your supplies and get rolling, call or e-mail Le Petit Artist directly at 610-779-9000 or www.lepetitartist.com and tell them which projects you're working on as well as your color preferences. They can put together a complete materials package (sans a few basic hardware store items that you can find close to home) and mail it to you. If you or a family member has a workshop, search there for things like a vise, a drill, and found objects for riveting projects—you'll be up and running in no time.

Because this collection has such a variety of project ideas, we decided that the beginning of each chapter was a good place to reveal a detailed materials list and photos of potentially unfamiliar items. Most of the items you'll use are standard to basic jewelry making. Your local bead shop can expose you to the myriad of beads, stones, and gems available, and help you choose bead combinations to suit your taste.

Wire-Wrapped Rings

*Y*ou can make a number of rings in one sitting, as they come together quickly and easily.

Tools

- round-nose pliers
- chain-nose pliers
- flush cutter
- ring mandrel

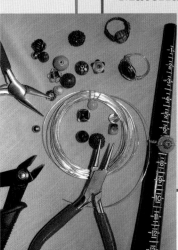

Materials

- 20-gauge craft wire—
  1 to $1^{1}/_{2}$ feet per ring (or
  use silver wire with a
  copper core—it stays
  nice and shiny)
- 10 to 15 mm disc beads
- 6 to 10 mm round beads
- bead cap

Disc-Shaped Bead Ring

1. On a ring mandrel, wrap wire around the appropriate line twice, marking a place slightly larger than the size you want your ring to be.

2. Turn the mandrel over, showing the grooved side. Thread both sides of the wire through a disc-shaped bead (the one with the hole on top) and push it toward the base of the wire to secure.

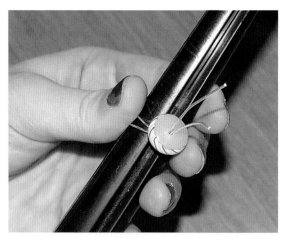

If using a glass bead, it may break when you feed the wire through, so proceed gently!

3. Thread a bead cap onto the wire in the same fashion as you did the bead.

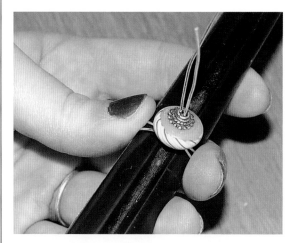

4. Pull one wire down one side and the other wire down the other side of the bead and bead cap.

5. Remove the ring from the mandrel.

6. Wrap one side of the wire around the base of the ring about five times, or more if you choose.

7. Trim excess wire with a flush cutter, keeping the flat side of the blade closest to the base of the wire. Try to get a clean cut without any sharp edges.

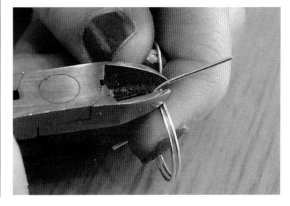

8. Repeat steps 4–7 on the other side of the bead with the remaining wire.

This is a simple yet eye-catching piece!

Variation 1: Swirled Ring

Add a swirl to the top of your bead instead of using a bead cap for a different look.

1. Wrap wire around the ring mandrel twice, and feed both ends through a disc bead.

2. Remove the ring from the mandrel.

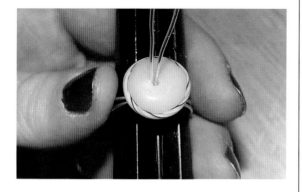

3. With round-nose pliers and your thumb and fingertips, wrap two wires around the tip of the pliers to begin a swirl shape.

4. Remove the pliers, and use your fingers to continue to swirl the wires in concentric circles on top of the bead.

5. Take one loose end of wire and wrap it around the base of the ring to secure it. Repeat with the other loose end of wire on the opposite side of the ring.

6. Trim off excess wire with the flush cutter.

The deep blue of this disc bead contrasts nicely with the wire-wrapped silver on top. The swirl need not be perfectly round—each bend makes the design unique.

1. Thread a globe-shaped bead to the middle of the wire, then place the bead in the groove of the mandrel.

2. Choose the ring size (go slightly larger than you need) on the mandrel and wrap the wire around it twice so that your loose ends are on either side.

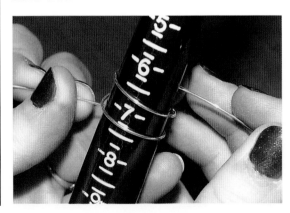

3. Place one wire above and one wire below the bead, then tighten to cradle the bead.

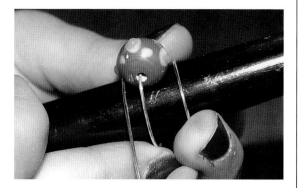

4. Wrap one of the loose wires around both the wires at the base, or shank, of the ring. Wrap around the shank twice to hold the bead in place and keep the ring from coming apart. Do the same on the other side.

5. Now you can remove the ring from the mandrel and tighten the wire with pliers. The ring is easier to work with once it's off the mandrel.

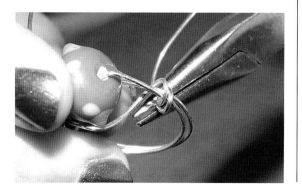

6. Wrap the wire around a few more times on both sides.

7. Trim off excess wire as close to the shank as possible. Always use the flat side of the flush cutter to get a smooth cut.

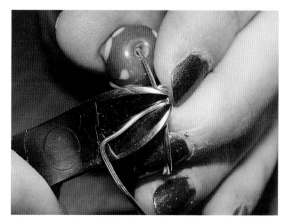

8. Push down the "tail" of the wire to bury the sharp edge.

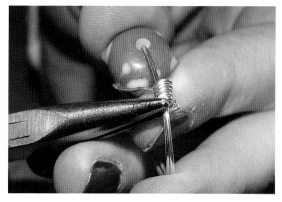

9. Return the ring to the mandrel to reshape the rounded part, as it may have become distorted as you wrapped the wire.

Even at this point, you can change the shape of your design by twisting the wire into a unique shape with your round- or chain-nose pliers.

These finished rings reveal the beauty of simple wire-wrapped designs with beads. Note the tight coils that secure each bead to the top of its ring.

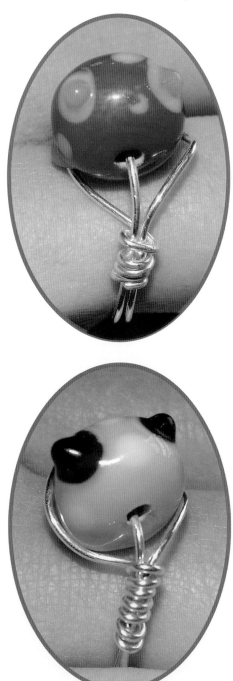

Fibula Pin

The fibula pin is a great project for beginners, as it is speedy and stylish to make. This pin bears its own simple distinction, yet offers a hint at the more complicated bending and beading to come.

Tools

- round-nose pliers
- chain-nose pliers
- flush cutter
- bench block
- chasing hammer
- jeweler's file

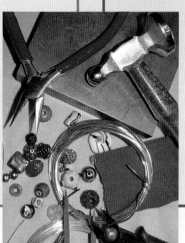

Materials

- 6 to 10 mm beads—various sizes and shapes
- charms (optional)
- #2 emery paper
- 18-gauge copper wire— 12 inches plus two or three 4-inch lengths
- 24-gauge craft wire— 6 inches

1. With round-nose pliers, make a small circle at one end of the 18-gauge wire.

2. Hold the small circle with chain-nose pliers, then bend the wire with your thumb and forefinger in a circular pattern, creating a swirl in the wire. Continue bending to make the swirl as large as you'd like.

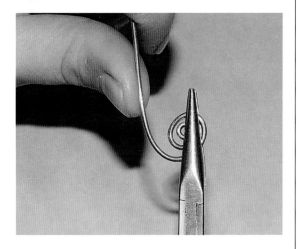

Copper is easily pliable, so have fun twirling your wire into a unique design.

3. Now bend the wire in the opposite direction, beginning to put a wave into the wire. Continue bending and twisting your wire into your own unique design.

4. After finishing the swirls and waves in your wire, use the round-nose pliers to begin forming a hook facing you straight on. This part will clasp over the top to close the pin.

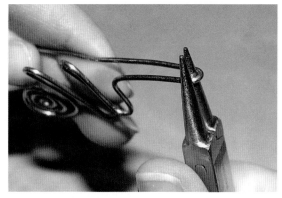

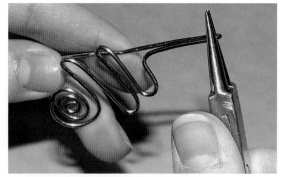

5. Pinch the looped end with chain-nose pliers.

6. Bend the wire about $1/2$ inch below the loop so the looped tip (or hook) is parallel to the plane of your swirled design.

7. Now take the 24-gauge wire and wrap it around the base of the hook with your thumb and forefinger. Tighten with chain-nose pliers if necessary.

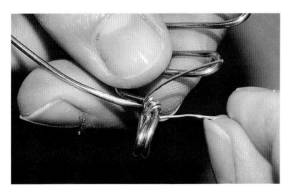

Here is how it will look from the side.

8. Continue to wrap the craft wire neatly along the straight side of the copper wire.

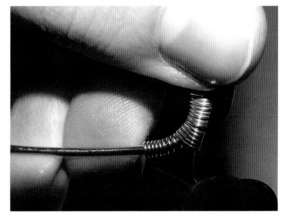

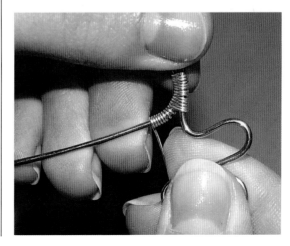

9. Trim excess with the flush cutter, keeping the sharp side of the cutter closest to the piece.

Always check to be sure that the flat side of your flush cutter blade is as close to the base of the jewelry piece as it can be to make a clean cut and a smooth finish.

Anywhere a wire is cut can potentially leave a sharp edge, so try to keep that edge tucked in and close to the wire that surrounds it.

10. Using a chasing hammer and a bench block, hammer out the wire to flatten it.

11. Use the flat side of the hammer for a smoother look . . .

. . . or the rounded end to create a more obvious textured, hammered look. Turn over the wire and hammer the other side in a similar fashion.

12. Choose a varied selection of beads to be added to the pin.

13. Add beads to the straight side of the wire.

Creating a Beaded Dangle

1. Using round-nose pliers, make a loop at the tip of a 4-inch length of copper wire.

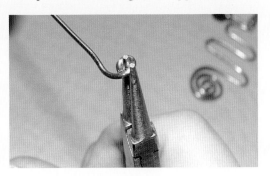

2. Continue to create a swirl using chain-nose pliers and your thumb and forefinger.

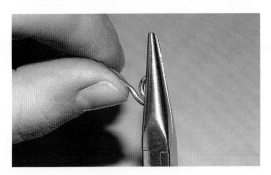

3. After finishing the small swirl, add beads and spacers as you wish, then use round-nose pliers to create a T-shaped loop at the mid-point of the wire.

4. Keeping the top T-shaped loop intact, use chain-nose pliers to wrap the wire around the straight, upper part of the dangle, filling in the remaining bare wire.

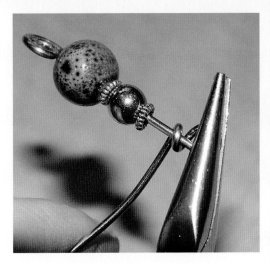

5. Once the bare wire is fully wrapped, trim the excess wire flush.

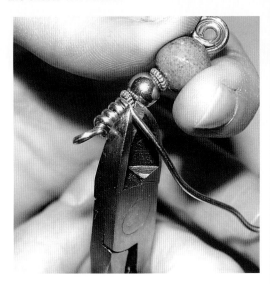

6. String the dangles along the pin for interest.

14. Secure the beads in place by forming a loop with round-nose pliers.

15. Let the wire on this side of the loop extend out straight, creating a flat top side for the pin.

16. Coil the copper around the nose of the pliers twice, allowing the unbeaded side of the wire to extend back across the length of the beaded section.

17. Cut the wire just past the top part of the clasp. This spot will be where the pin clasps.

18. Use a file to sharpen the tip of the wire to a fine point.

19. Then go over it again with emery paper to smooth it out. This step will make the wire glide easily through the knitted or woven fabric of your garment.

You can use craft wire for this project if you prefer a silver-toned finish, but beware that when the tip is filed to a point, the copper core of the wire will be revealed. If you want to avoid this two-toned tip, just stick with copper wire.

Avoid wearing the fibula pin on silk or other finely woven fabrics, as it may leave a hole where it is inserted. Opt instead for knitted or woven fabrics, such as sweaters, heavier blazers, or jackets.

Barrette

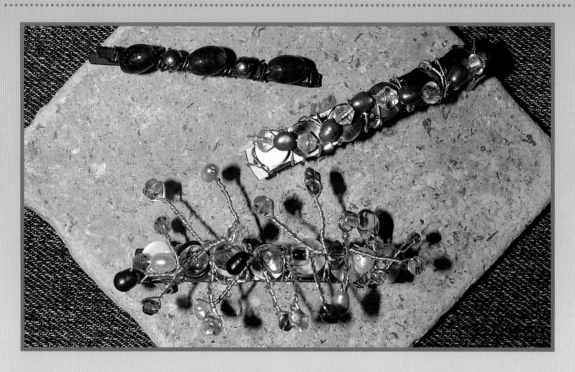

*Y*ou can use a barrette of any shape or size for this project. A longer one is probably easiest to work with, as you will be going back and forth across its surface with beads and wire.

Tools
- round-nose pliers
- chain-nose pliers
- flush cutter

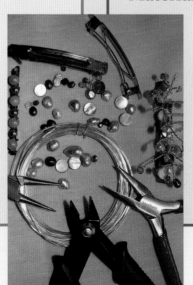

Materials
- 24-gauge craft wire—1 yard
- 1 barrette—large size
- 8 to 10 mm mother-of-pearl disc beads
- semiprecious beads: Czech crystals, Swarovski, or fresh-water pearls (8 mm, 6 mm, and 4 mm)

1. Secure the wire by threading one end through and wrapping it around one of the holes in the barrette.

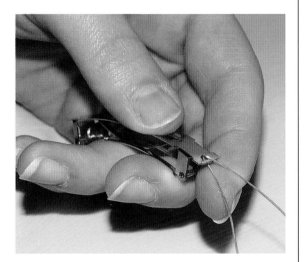

3. String one mother-of-pearl bead and secure it on top of the barrette by wrapping the wire around the base.

2. After wrapping and tightening the wire, cut off excess at the back of the barrette, and push the cut end to the underside.

4. Thread the wire through the wrapped wire to secure it, then continue with a second flat bead.

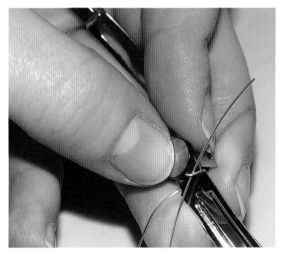

Do not wrap wire around the arched spring of the barrette.

5. Continue to secure beads along the entire length of the barrette by wrapping the whole base or by threading the wire through the holes in the metal. As long as you're securing the beads, you're doing it right!

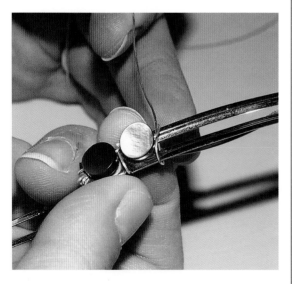

6. Tighten the wrapped wire using chain-nose pliers.

Semiprecious beads have smaller holes than others, so remember to use these with narrower wire, such as the 24-gauge wire used here.

7. Once you have reached the end of the barrette, thread the wire through the top hole.

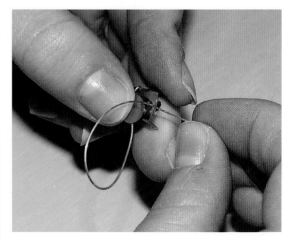

Now that the flat beads are covering the length of the metal barrette, you can begin surrounding them with 8 mm, 6 mm, and 4 mm beads—shiny ones work well here.

8. Bring the wire back to the top end of the barrette. String a few beads and anchor the wire by wrapping wire around the back, or bottom, of the barrette.

To add height to the piece, leave a bit of wire showing rather than letting a bead fall flush with the base. Then turn the bead with your thumb and forefinger, making the wire twist up.

9. Continue adding beads to the wire, twisting and securing, until you reach the opposite end of the barrette and you're pleased with the design. If you want more beadwork throughout the length of the barrette, work your way back in the opposite direction.

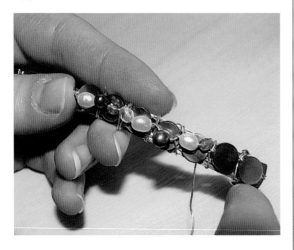

10. Once again, thread the wire through the hole at the end of the barrette to secure this line of beads.

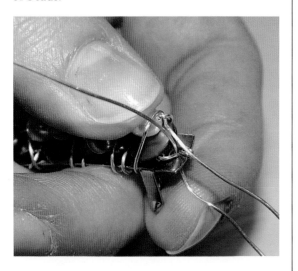

11. Wrap the wire a few times at the end of the barrette, trim the excess with the flush cutter, and bury the tip to finish.

Your choice of beads and the way you wrap wire can make your barrettes range from classic to funky.

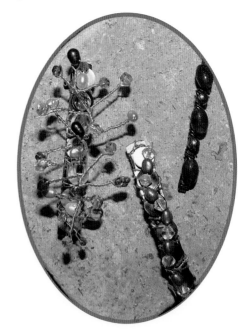

Swarovski Crystal Cluster Earrings

Choose crystals to complement a formal gown, then wear your earrings again with jeans—they are just as stylish with either ensemble.

Tools
- round-nose pliers
- chain-nose pliers
- flush cutter

Materials
- 2 French hooks
- 28 headpins
- jump rings
- 32 Swarovski crystals, various colors:
    - 2 bicone shape 8 mm
    - 24 bicone shape 6 mm
    - 6 bicone shape 4 mm

You'll use the following materials for this project: French hooks, Swarovski crystals in various colors and sizes, headpins, and jump rings.

Swarovski crystals draw the eye with their multifaceted, sparkling surfaces.

1. Pick up a headpin and string an 8 mm crystal on it.

2. Cut off the headpin about a fingertip's length above the bead. (You could also bend the headpin first, then cut—try both ways and do what's easiest for you.)

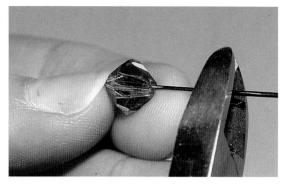

3. With round-nose pliers, create a loop at the top of the headpin and squeeze the pliers to tighten it.

The finished loop should be flush with the bead.

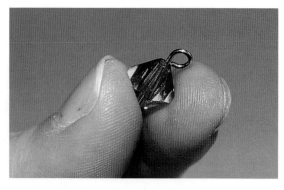

4. Repeat thirty-one times, moving from largest to smallest, so each crystal is on its own looped headpin. Divide the crystals into two even piles—sixteen crystals for each earring.

5. Twist open a jump ring using chain-nose pliers and your fingertips.

Don't simply pry open a jump ring evenly on both sides, as this can put too much strain on the ring, causing it to break. Twist it open—and closed—instead.

6. Clamp one side of the jump ring with chain-nose pliers. Place a large crystal on the ring first, then a small crystal. Be sure the large crystal is on the bottom.

8. If you have three bead loops on a jump ring, you want the smallest one to hang on the outside when assembled.

7. Add a few more beads to the jump ring. There's no official pattern here, but you want to vary your choices: avoid using two beads of the same color on one jump ring; vary bead sizes and the number of beads per ring as well.

9. Add as many beads to one jump ring as you wish. More beads will make for a thicker, wider piece.

10. Close up the jump ring by twisting the tips together again with your fingertips. (The pliers will hold the opposite side in place.)

11. Continue to load jump rings with bead loops, then join two loaded jump rings. This pairing will make the earring begin to dangle.

12. Continue making a chain with jump rings to reach the desired length of your earring, or until you're used up all your bead loops for that earring.

13. Open the loop of a French hook by first pulling the ball up and then twisting open the loop (as you did for the jump rings earlier).

Be careful not to bend a French hook loop too much, as it is delicate and may break.

14. Attach the beaded cluster to the hook so that the 8 mm crystal hangs at the bottom, close up the loop, and allow the ball to fall back to its resting place.

15. Repeat steps 5–14 to create the matching earring.

It's nice to begin with classic shades such as yellow and red, then add contrasting colors for interest. On this cluster, the purple and green beads really stand out.

Wire-Loop Earrings

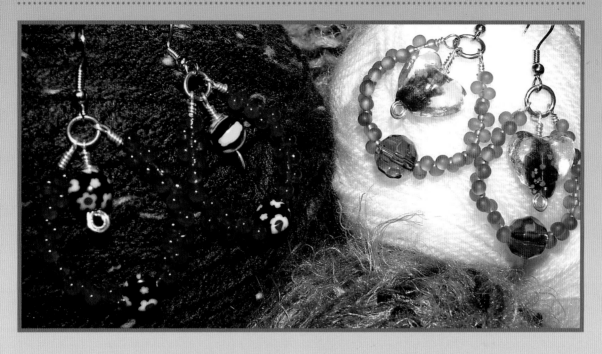

*C*hoose the large bead that will hang in the center first, then plan the accompanying smaller beads around it, similar to framing a photograph.

Tools

- round-nose pliers
- chain-nose pliers
- flush cutter

Materials

- 22-gauge craft wire—two 8-inch strips plus two 3-inch strips
- 68 drop beads (3.4 mm) (teardrop-shaped beads with hole on top)
- 2 round beads (8 to 9 mm)
- 2 beads (8 to 15 mm) to hang in center of loops: round, oval, heart, or any shape is fine
- 2 French hooks

1. With round-nose pliers, make a loop about 1 inch from one end of an 8-inch strip of wire.

2. Wrap the short end of the wire two or three times around the base of the loop.

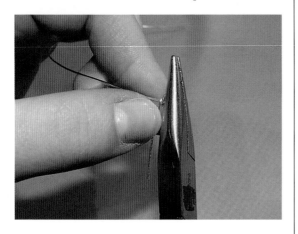

3. Trim off any excess.

Have your drop beads counted out and ready.

4. String seventeen drop beads on the wire.

5. Put on a larger bead. This bead will hang at the bottom center of the loop upon finishing.

6. String seventeen more drop beads onto the wire.

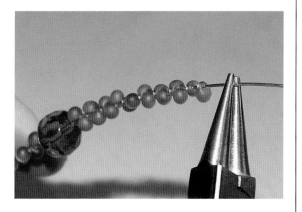

7. With round-nose pliers, bend the open end of the wire into a loop a fingertip's width from where the beads end.

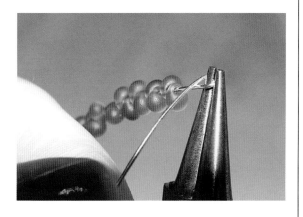

8. Hold the loop with chain-nose pliers . . .

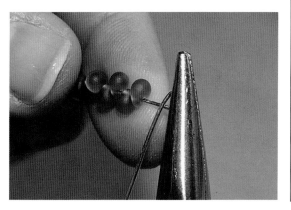

. . . and wrap the wire around the base two or three times.

9. Cut off the excess flush with the base.

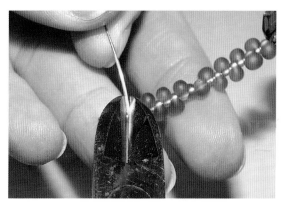

10. Pinch the wrapped wire with chain-nose pliers to be sure the trimmed edge doesn't stick out.

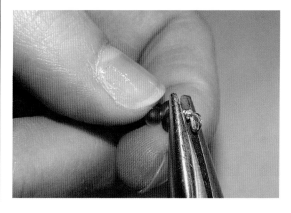

The beads should be fairly tight on the wire at this point.

11. Bend the wire into a teardrop shape with your fingers.

12. Pick up the 3-inch wire . . .

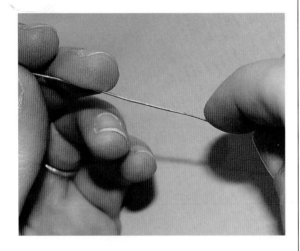

. . . and make a loop at the tip with round-nose pliers.

13. Hold the loop with chain-nose pliers and bend the wire into a small swirl with your thumb and forefinger.

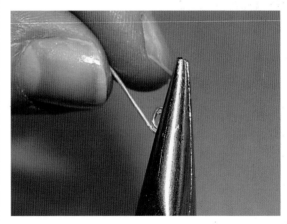

The swirl should be just a couple loops thick.

14. String the bead that you want to hang in the center of the earring here.

15. Place the round-nose pliers a little more than half a fingertip above the top of the bead . . .

. . . and make a loop with the wire.

16. Hold the loop with chain-nose pliers and wrap the base two or three times to secure the bead in place.

17. Trim the excess wire flush and bend in the sharp edge.

18. With chain-nose pliers and your thumb and forefinger, open a jump ring by twisting (not pulling) apart the two sides.

19. Put one side of the loop on the jump ring.

20. Then add the center dangle.

21. Then add the other side of the loop.

22. Twist the jump ring to close.

Here is the completed loop.

23. Pick up a French hook, lift the ball that falls over the base of the loop, open the loop by twisting, and attach the beaded loop.

Here is the completed earring.

24. Twist back to close the French hook.

25. Repeat the entire process to create the second earring.

Cabochon Pendant

A cabochon is a stone that has been shaped into a form, often oval, with a rounded top and a flat bottom. Because of the size and shape of cabochons, they can be easily mounted within a creative arrangement of wire, making an eye-catching jewelry piece. This pendant is popular because you can create lovely stone jewelry without soldering.

Here, we will wrap a typical large, oval cabochon. It's best to start with this shape and size and save uneven shapes, such as teardrop-shaped cabochons, for when you've mastered wrapping this one.

Tools

- round-nose pliers
- chain-nose pliers
- flush cutter
- vise
- wire twister
- alligator clips

Materials

- 40 x 30 oval cabochon
  - 20-gauge silver craft wire—two 1-foot lengths
  - 24-gauge silver craft wire—3 feet
  - 24-gauge copper wire—1 foot
  - chain, collar, ribbon, or leather cord to attach pendant
  - various small beads

1. Cut about 1 foot of the 24-gauge silver wire, then clamp the 24-gauge copper and silver wire about 1 inch deep in a vise, so they hold firmly. Set aside the remainder of the 24-gauge silver wire for later use.

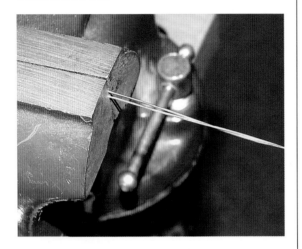

2. At the opposite end, clamp the wires into a wire twister. Be sure the wires are clamped in securely, then lock the clamp.

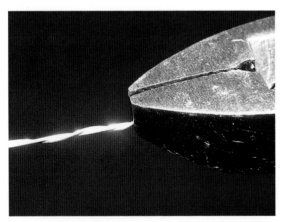

3. Pull on the twister's back lever with one hand while allowing the handles to spin in a circle through your other loosely gripped hand. You control how loose or tight you want the twist. The wire will tell you if it's too tight by kinking. If this happens, just loosen and try again.

Here is a loosely twisted wire.

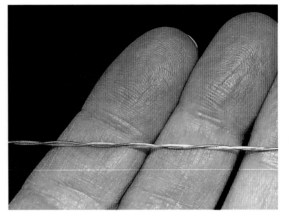

This wire is more tightly twisted.

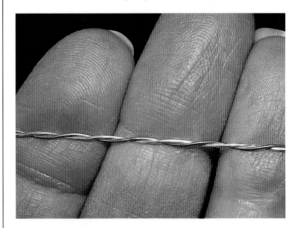

You can buy wire that's already twisted, but you can save money by twisting it yourself. This bit of hand-work also allows more creativity, be-cause you can mix copper and silver wire as shown here. Most pretwisted wire combines two strands of the same type and color.

4. When the wire is twisted tight enough to your liking, remove the wire from the vise. The wire should be wrapped tightly enough that it stays twisted.

5. Lay all three pieces of wire (the two 20-gauge lengths and the twisted length) on the table with the twisted wire in between the two pieces of 20-gauge wire.

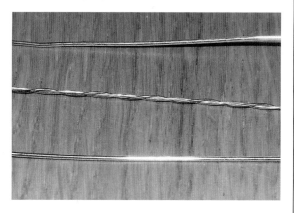

6. Keep the twisted wire in the middle, then clip both ends with the alligator clips, about one palm's width apart from one another. Be sure all pieces are secured in the teeth of the clips.

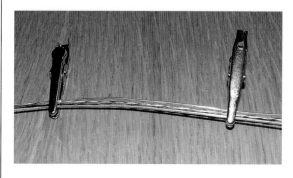

7. Cut a 4-inch piece of 24-gauge silver craft wire and wrap it around the center of the other wires, keeping them in order, with the twisted wire in the center.

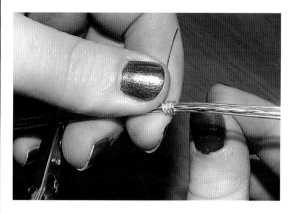

You can use your pliers to keep the wires flat as you wrap.

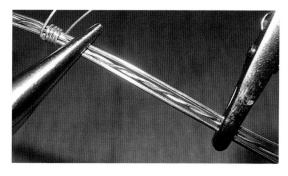

8. Continue to coil the single wire around the grouped wires about eight times.

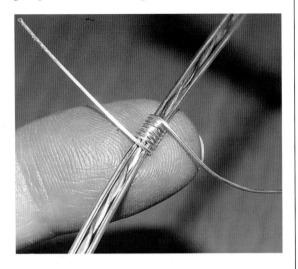

9. When you are finished wrapping the 24-gauge wire, snip the edge flush. This edge should face the surface of the cabochon so it won't show on the finished piece.

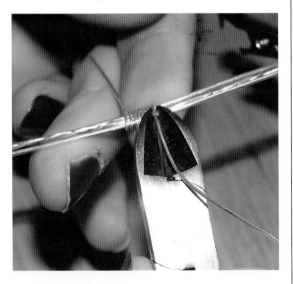

10. Cut another 4-inch piece of 24-gauge silver wire. To the left of the first coil (about an inch), coil the single wire around the grouped wire about eight times. Again, cut the wire at the inside to hide the end of the wire.

11. Begin to bend the wire around the cabochon. Keeping the wires stacked, move one clip up to allow more wire around the stone.

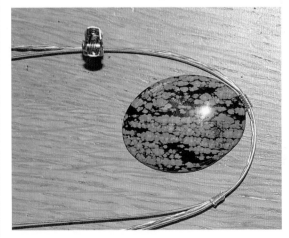

12. Now remove the clip from the opposite side and wrap a 4-inch piece of wire around the wires to the right of the first coil (about an inch). Keep the wires flat and stacked for a clean appearance when they are attached to the stone.

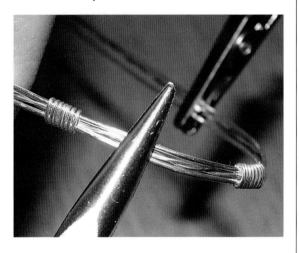

13. After bending the wire to hug the cabochon, the two wrapped sides should fall at the midpoint of each side. If they aren't too tight, you can slide the wraps up or down as needed to center them.

14. Hold the wire around the stone and begin to crease it into an L shape at the top of both sides. This is the top of the piece, where you will make the bail.

15. Pick up the wire piece, setting the cabochon aside. Take the back wire from one side and wrap it around where you made the creases. Wrap around all five wires one or two times—just enough to hold the pieces together.

16. Put the cabochon back in the center of the stacked wire. It should fit snugly.

As you put it in, begin to pull the bottom wire in toward the center of the back to secure the cabochon. Do the same with the front side.

17. Next, pull down the wires for the curlicues that will adorn the face of the cabochon. Pick three wires to pull down toward the front, including the twisted wire. Make the bail with the two remaining wires or "rabbit ears."

Make a relatively large bail, so it can be worn on either a slide or a chain.

18. Hold both strands of the rabbit ears together with round-nose pliers, about $1/2$ inch above the top of the cabochon.

19. Bend one wire down toward the back of the cabochon, then make a notch or crease at the base where you will wrap the bail.

20. Repeat with the other wire to form a similar crease for the other side of your bail.

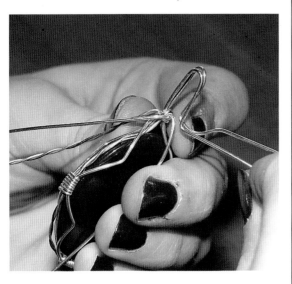

21. With the same wire you used to wrap around the strands, bring the wire around the back to catch the notch you just created.

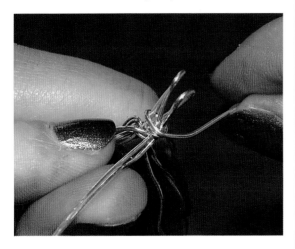

22. Wrap as generously as you wish, as this is part of your design.

23. Cut excess wire hanging below the bail with a flush cutter, as close to the base as you can. If enough wire is left sticking out, you can bend it inside the rabbit ears so it won't catch on anything.

24. Gather the beads you'd like to use on the curlicues. This photo shows a few more than you'll need.

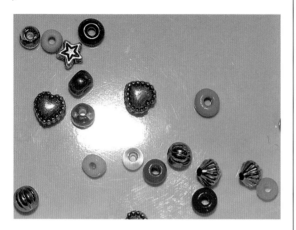

25. Cut off the remaining three wires so they won't hang below the stone when curled. Cut each one a different length for variety.

26. Feed a few beads onto two of the twisted wires—your design determines the exact number.

27. To anchor the beads, wrap the twisted wire around the round-nose pliers, making a small loop.

28. Hold the loop with chain-nose pliers and use your finger to twist it into a swirl.

29. With round-nose pliers, create a corkscrew with the other twisted wire, add beads along its length, and secure it to one of the side wires that holds the cabochon.

Here are the finished twisted wires.

Do this on both the front and back of the cabochon.

30. The third strand can be coiled or beaded. Use chain-nose pliers to tuck in the bottom of the wire.

31. Once all three wires have been beaded or coiled, take the chain-nose pliers and twist the wires on the back of the piece at all four securing points—where they are bent midway to secure the cabochon—to tighten them.

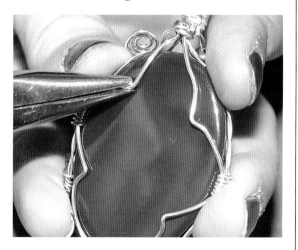

The third strand, a single craft wire, was twisted into a swirl on this piece.

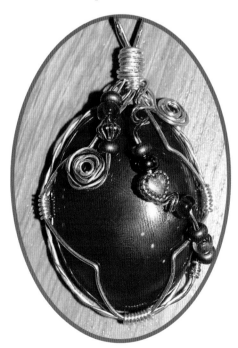

Tri-Strand Cluster Necklace

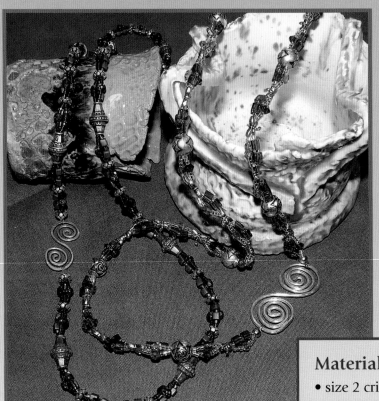

The delicate beadwork in this design seems complicated at first, but once your first cluster or two are strung, the rest of the necklace simply requires repetition. The final result will have everyone admiring your style and creativity.

Tools

- round-nose pliers
- chain-nose pliers
- flush cutter
- bench block
- chasing hammer or ball-peen hammer
- crimping tool for size 2 crimp beads

Materials

- size 2 crimp beads or crimp tubes
- crimp covers
- 16-gauge wire—1 foot
- Beadalon, Soft Flex, or Tigertail thread—three strands, 1 1/2 yards each
- 28 spacers (6 mm)
- 9 spacers (9 to 10 mm)
- 4 x 4 mm cube beads—1 tube
- size 11 delicas
- 36 Czech crystals (4 mm)
- 36 Swarovski crystals (4 mm)

Wire Swirl

1. Make a loop at one end of the wire using round-nose pliers.

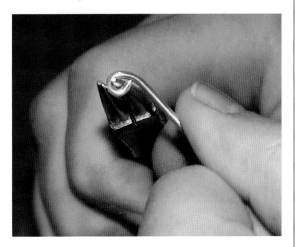

2. Use chain-nose pliers and your thumb and forefinger to twist a tight spiral shape into the wire, using nearly half the wire.

3. Repeat steps 1 and 2 on the opposite side of the wire, twisting the opposite way, to create an S-shaped piece.

4. Flatten the spirals by hammering the piece on the bench block. Use the flat side of the hammer for a smooth look or the rounded side for a textured look. Turn over the wire and hammer the other side.

Necklace

Crimp covers—a relatively new invention—will cover your crimps and add a decorative touch at either side of your clasp.

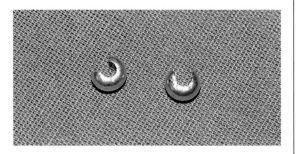

1. Slide a crimp bead over all three strands of thread near one end.

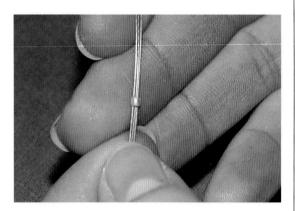

2. Thread the three strands through the outer ring of one of the spirals of the clasp.

3. Feed all three strands back through the crimp bead, forming a loop. Push the crimp bead up so it is close to the wire swirl.

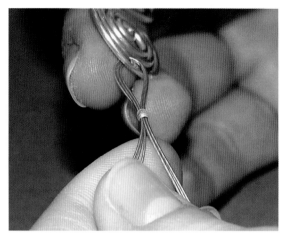

4. Gently squeeze the crimp bead with the back notch on the crimping tool, forming a U shape. Rotate one-quarter turn, making a crescent shape like a backwards C.

5. Using the crimping tool, hold the crimp bead in the front notch and gently squeeze the crimp bead again on top of itself, forming a ball shape.

6. Cover the crimp bead with a crimp cover.

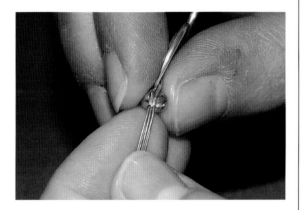

7. Close and tighten the crimp cover with chain-nose pliers.

The closed crimp cover.

8. On the first strand, string three delicas, one Swarovski crystal, and three more delicas.

Before cutting the three short ends of the thread, you will feed them under the beaded strands. The crystals and beads have holes wide enough to fit two widths of thread through them.

9. Feed one strand of short thread under these beads, then trim the excess flush.

10. On the second strand, string three delicas, one Czech crystal, and three more delicas. Feed a second strand of short thread under these beads and trim the excess flush.

11. On the third strand, string one delica, one cube, one delica, one cube, and one delica, for a total of five beads, then hide the end of the third short strand by feeding it through these beads. Trim the excess flush.

12. Here are all three strands, with the short ends threaded through and trimmed. The thread is now secure and ready to be beaded into the necklace.

13. String a small spacer over all three strands.

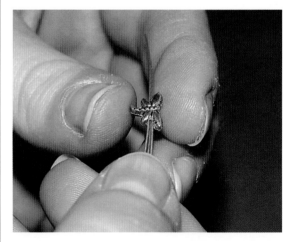

14. Press the spacer tightly up next to the beaded cluster.

This project calls for eight sections of four clusters and two sections of two clusters. This pattern will create a 14-inch necklace, approximately. You can modify the number of sections and the size of the swirl to your liking. Just remember to make it long enough to go over the head—there's no clasp to open and close the piece.

15. Make one more cluster, following the same pattern as the first cluster.

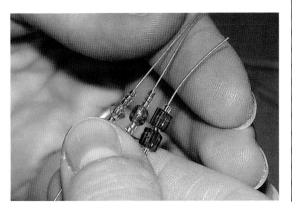

16. Then, string on a large spacer.

17. Press the spacer in tightly next to the bead cluster.

18. Continue making clusters, but wait until after the fourth cluster to attach a large spacer.

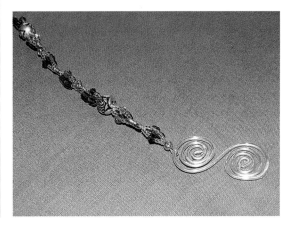

If your fingers are agile, try stringing all three strands at once. This technique will help you keep track of which strand you're working on.

19. Make eight sections of four clusters.

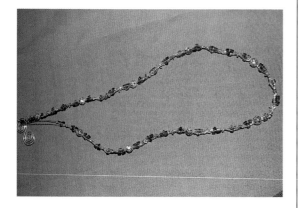

As you continue to string beads, make sure each cluster is pulled tight.

20. Finish with two additional clusters for symmetry. Thread all three strands through a crimp bead.

21. Feed the three strands through the outer loop of the other side of the spiral wire swirl.

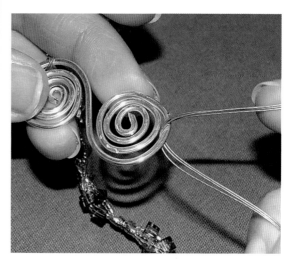

22. Feed the threads back through the crimp bead to form a loop.

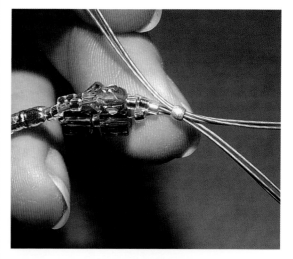

23. Find three good places to tuck in each of the three short strands, weaving them under three or four beads.

24. Pull each strand to tighten. This method will get the strands nice and close to the wire swirl.

25. Tighten the crimp with the crimping tool.

26. Trim the excess threads flush.

27. Attach the crimp cover over the crimp bead.

28. Tighten with chain-nose pliers.

You could substitute larger glass beads for the metal ones for a different look.

This necklace does not have a clasp—it can simply be put on over your head. You can make this piece as colorful or subdued as you want to match a variety of favorite outfits.

Twist-and-Wrap Bracelet

Wire is used like thread in this project, binding many beads together. Large beads and imprecise wrapping give it a funky look. Use semiprecious or glass beads to fill in blank spaces—they are cost-effective. This project can get expensive depending on the number of beads that are used.

Tools

- round-nose pliers
- chain-nose pliers
- flush cutter
- bench block
- chasing hammer

Materials

- 22-gauge wire—3 or more lengths, 1 1/2 feet each
- 16-gauge wire—6 inches
- 5 or 6 beads (10 to 15 mm)
- 15 beads (6 to 8 mm)— use different shapes, sizes, and colors for texture
- 100 beads—0/8, 0/6 seed beads, cubes, rounds, and nuggets to add texture
- add silver or gold beads for sparkle

§ **55**

1. About 2 inches from one end of 22-gauge wire, string a large bead.

2. Loop wire over the top of the bead, then tie a knot in the wire to anchor the bead.

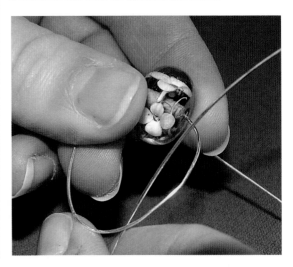

3. Continue stringing and knotting large beads about 1 inch apart, for a total of five to six large beads (modify this for a larger- or smaller-than-average bracelet). Make sure all beads on this first baseline sit upright in a row.

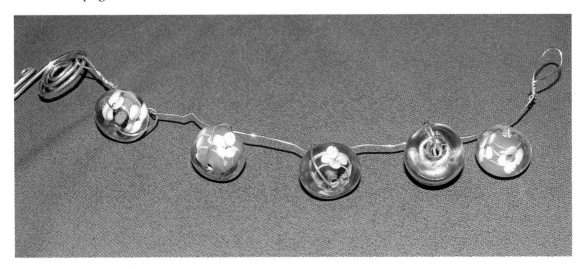

You will have to help the wire through the bead holes with your fingers, as it is thick and a little stubborn.

Make the bracelet long enough to encircle your wrist minus $^1/_2$ inch— the S hook will add that much length. Err on the side of too long. The bracelet can be shortened by twisting and wrapping later if need be.

4. Leave 2 inches at the opposite end, and cut the wire. Put this piece aside.

5. Begin creating an S hook by bending one end of the 16-gauge wire at the back of the round-nose pliers into a loop.

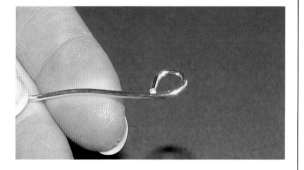

6. Use chain-nose pliers to continue the spiral.

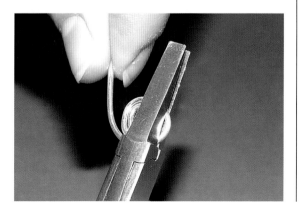

7. Once you are close to the midpoint of the wire, hold the spiral toward your body with the round-nose pliers and begin to bend the wire away from your body. Do not bend all the way— just until the wire resembles a pelican.

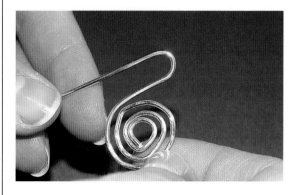

8. With the flatter side of the flush cutters toward you, clip the wire, leaving about $1^1/_2$ inches.

9. Using the front tip of the round-nose pliers, roll the end of the wire into a loop.

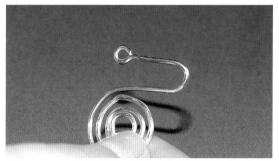

10. After you shape the top loop into a decorative swirl, the S hook is ready for hammering.

11. With the flat side of the chasing hammer, flatten the S hook. It's helpful to hammer both sides equally, so as not to weaken the wire too much in one space.

12. Feed the S hook onto the end of the baseline wire and make a loop. Pinch the loop with chain-nose pliers. Use your fingers to twist enough wire around the baseline to secure the wire—about two or three turns.

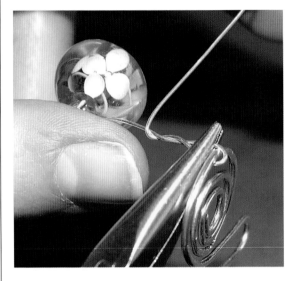

13. Tighten the wrapped wire and trim the excess.

14. Repeat making a loop at the other end without using a clasp—this will attach to the S hook on the opposite side—and trim the excess. Make sure your loop is large enough to fit the S hook through so it will clasp.

You will use beads of varied colors, shapes, and sizes to fill the spaces between the large beads on the baseline.

15. Wrap a second length of 22-gauge wire under the first bead on the baseline to anchor it. Feed a medium bead and a few bead chips onto this wire. These beads will begin to fill in the space between the large beads on the baseline.

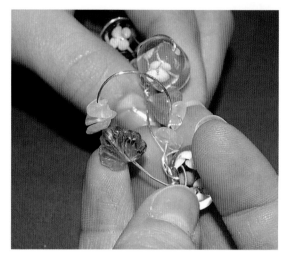

16. Make an arc with the wire and wrap it under the second bead on the baseline, tying a knot to fasten it the same way as you did the large beads on the baseline. The arc is important because you want to have "floating beads" that can move along the wire. (The floating beads become important later in the process.)

Here is how the second line will look once the beads are anchored.

17. Repeat this process all the way across the bracelet.

> The size of beads, what beads you begin with, and what beads you fill in with will control how dense your bracelet will be. Try not to leave any bare holes along the length of the bracelet.

18. With chain-nose pliers, grab the wire on one side of a floating bead and twist the wire clockwise to tighten the bead in place. Repeat this twist on the other side of the bead if it is still floating. Continue to twist and tighten in this fashion all the way around the bracelet.

This twisting and tightening of the wire is similar to the process used to hold the cabochon in place, as shown on pages 42–43.

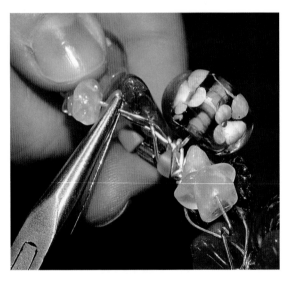

19. Here is the bracelet with three strands beaded and the beads tightened and secure.

20. If you have enough excess wire, go back through the bracelet in the opposite direction. Otherwise, begin a new line. This time, you can use small beads.

The small beads help the bracelet look finished by filling in the small spaces along the wire.

21. When you string a new bead, weave the wire back through the hole of a bead already on the bracelet to anchor it.

If you are using beads with a finish, such as faux pearls, construct your bracelet carefully so you don't chip the surface.

22. As you continue to bead and twist wire, look for "naked" patches on the bracelet where you think a bead can fill the space, then add it there. The wire must be tight and strong.

Even after you're done adding beads to the bracelet, you can go back through the piece with just wire and tighten it to make the whole bracelet tighter and secure.

Twist in the same direction throughout to limit the strain on the wire; 22-gauge can snap. If this happens, just twist the wire inside the bracelet and continue with a new piece. Keep the beads tight, and the bracelet will be fine.

If your bracelet gets too heavy at the end where you anchor the wire, just switch to the other end to begin. Avoid a heavy-ended bracelet by working back and forth throughout the process.

24. Plan to run wire through the bracelet many times. Weave and bead liberally to make the piece thick and strong. Twisting the wires strengthens the whole bracelet. Three passes will not make a strong bracelet!

Your bracelet should have an obvious top side and bottom side: the bottom side should be flat, and the top full with beads.

You can wrap over previously wrapped wire to reach a sparsely beaded section of the bracelet, then fill it in with beads when you get there.

25. Bend the bracelet into a circular shape, fasten the loop to the S hook, and your bracelet is complete.

23. At the base of the bracelet on both ends, wrap the wire liberally to be sure it securely anchors the wire that runs through the bracelet. This bulky collection of wires serves an important purpose: it holds your bracelet together!

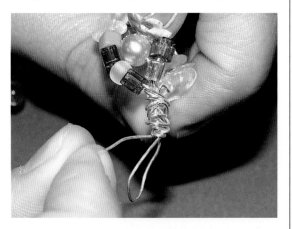

Coil Bracelet

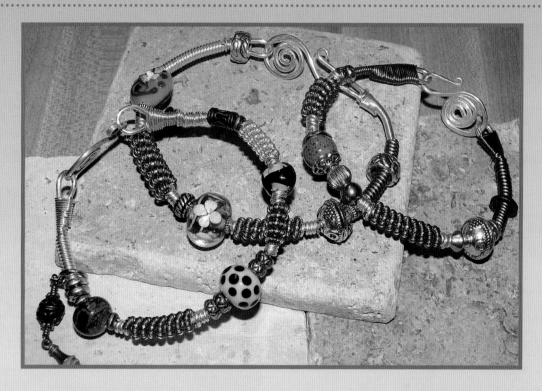

This ultrastylish bracelet is a sophisticated take on heavy metal. An average-sized bracelet is $7^1/2$ inches long; a bangle is 8 to $8^1/2$ inches. This piece is just as stunning either way.

Tools

- round-nose pliers
- chain-nose pliers
- flush cutter
- Coiling Gizmo
- bench block
- chasing hammer

Materials

- 22-gauge copper wire—1 yard, plus $1^1/2$ feet
- 18-gauge craft wire—three 15-inch lengths
- 14-gauge craft wire—15 inches
- 6 to 15 mm beads (with holes large enough to fit 14-gauge wire)
- metal rings

When working with wire, it's better to have it too long rather than come up short.

Coils

1. Begin wrapping one end of the long copper wire around the loop of the Coiling Gizmo to anchor the wire.

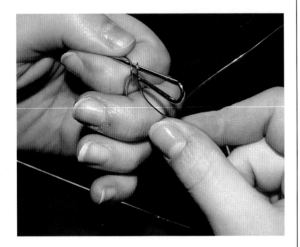

2. Wrap three times.

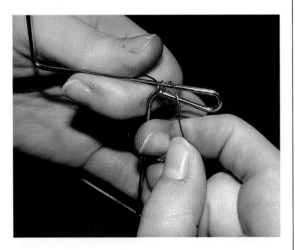

3. Let the wire hang down from the loop, and insert the Gizmo into its bracket.

4. Hold the long end of the wire against the flat side of the bracket with your thumb and begin to twist the loop's "handle" to make the coil.

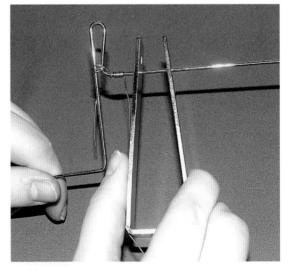

Make sure the copper wire wraps evenly, one layer at a time, so it doesn't overlap.

5. When wire is fully coiled, about 5 inches, trim the wire wrapped around the anchoring loop to release the coil.

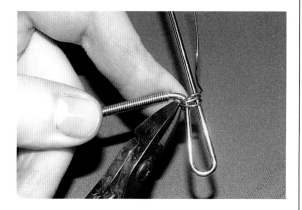

6. Slide the coil off the Gizmo and trim the excess.

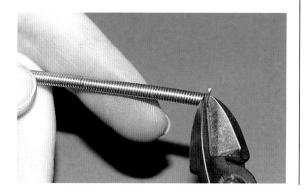

If you have wrapped the coil very tightly, you may need to unwind a bit to loosen it from the Gizmo.

7. Slide the coil onto the 18-gauge craft wire to measure: the craft wire should be about three times as long as the coil.

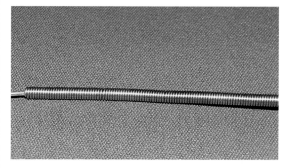

8. Wrap the craft wire onto the Coiling Gizmo.

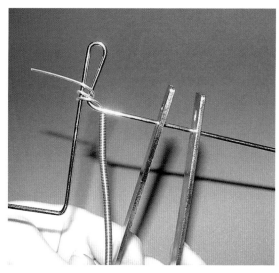

9. Begin to turn the handle to twist the coil into another coil.

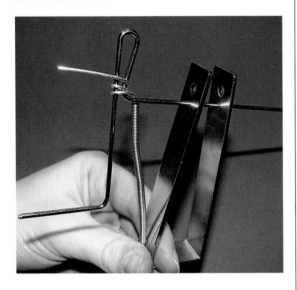

10. You will create a thinner, coiled craft wire segment with a larger copper segment in the middle. Continue twisting just past the end of the copper segment, and trim any excess wire flush. Slide the coil off the Gizmo, then make another coil like the one you just completed.

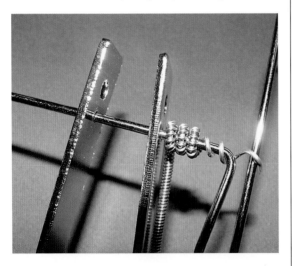

Alternate method for beginners:

Thread 18-gauge craft wire through the bottom hole of the Coiling Gizmo.

Coil copper wire right around the craft wire, then trim away the loose part.

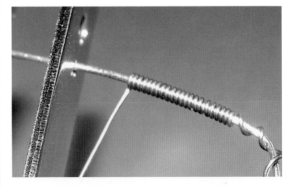

You can make coils ahead of time for later use in bracelets.

Here is the difference between a coil wrapped around a Gizmo, which is larger, and one that is wrapped right onto the craft wire.

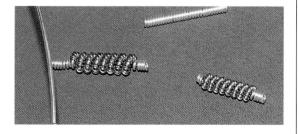

11. To create a plain coil, wrap the wire right around the Gizmo, without threading it onto the craft wire.

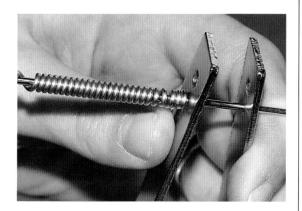

12. Put the coils aside and cut about 8 inches of the 14-gauge craft wire. Bend one end into a teardrop-shaped loop using round-nose pliers. Keep the loop wide enough on the inside to allow the clasp to feed through it later.

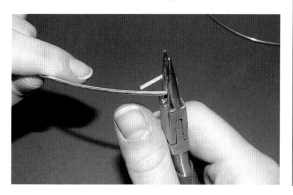

13. Wrap a 6-inch length of 22-gauge copper wire over the base of the loop and above and below it a bit, creating a smooth "neck" between the loop and the bracelet.

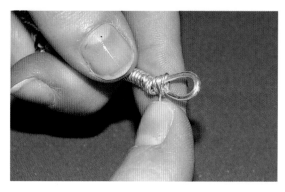

14. String the beads and coils onto the wire in the pattern you wish to create.

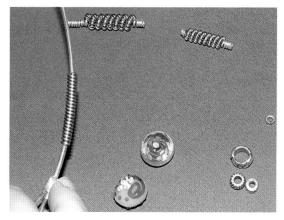

15. You can string larger ring beads over the narrow coils to add movement.

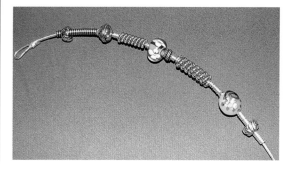

16. After all beads are strung, use round-nose pliers to make a loop at the unfinished end, leaving enough wire to enclose it with wrapped wire.

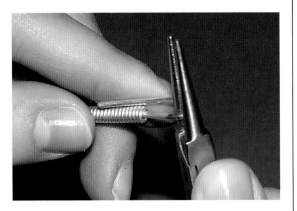

17. Trim the excess with a flush cutter.

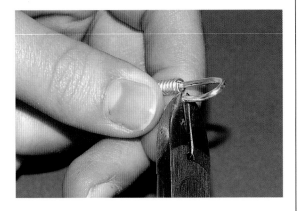

18. Wrap a 6-inch length of 22-gauge copper wire around the neck of the loop, starting at the base of the loop and wrapping liberally around it.

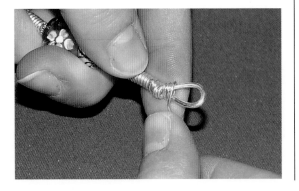

19. Once wire covers the base of the loop, leaving a nice gradual slope from hook to bracelet, trim any excess wire and bury the sharp end of wire as well as you can.

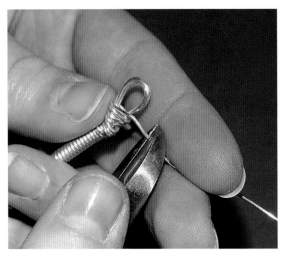

20. Bend the beaded wire into the shape of a bangle bracelet.

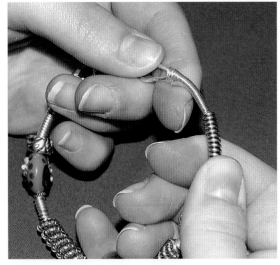

The ends should not quite meet.

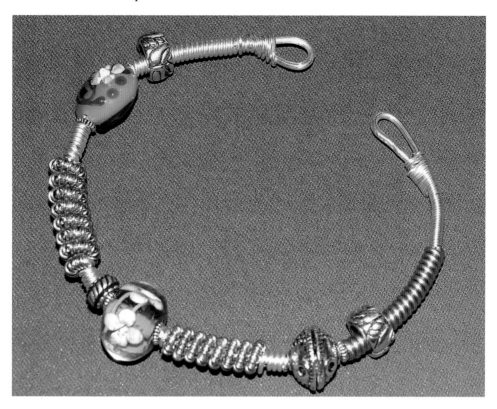

If you are dissatisfied with the way your wrapping looks, you can remove and redo it. Use the same wire only if it isn't too noticeably bent. Otherwise, just start again with new wire.

21. With the remaining 14-gauge wire (about $4^1/2$ inches), use a chasing hammer to flatten one end. Turn over the wire and hammer the other side.

22. Make a small loop on the flattened end using round-nose pliers.

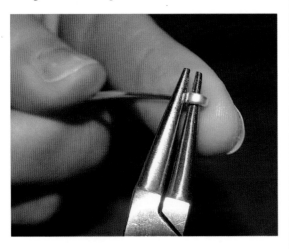

23. Bend the wire about ¹/₂ inch from the loop in the opposite direction.

Now decide how big you want your clasp to be. If you want to keep it smaller, cut off some of the wire so the spiral you create will be more compact.

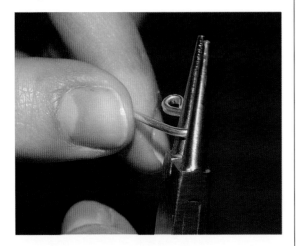

24. On the other end of the wire, make a small loop in the opposite direction. Begin bending the wire into a spiral.

25. Using chain-nose pliers and your thumb and forefinger, continue to spiral around. This heavier gauge wire will take a bit more work to bend.

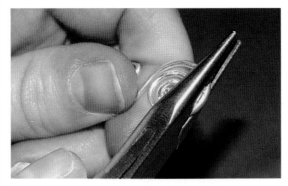

26. When you near the outer edge of the coil, make the space between coils wider so that the clasp will fit on easily.

27. Hammer the clasp to flatten it. You may want to keep the arched part round and just flatten the spiral. Use the flat side of the hammer to keep the surface uniform; the rounded tip leaves a textured appearance. Turn over the wire and hammer the other side.

Hammering makes the wire harder, so be sure the wire is where you want it before you flatten it.

28. Slide the clasp onto the loop.

29. Tighten the spiral beyond the loop so it stays secure on the bracelet.

30. Clasp the other end, and you have a completed coil bracelet.

If you prefer a larger, bangle-style bracelet that you can slide on and off your wrist, simply create a larger clasp.

Knitted Bracelet

The finished bracelet is flexible and will roll over your hand onto your wrist—no fastening required.

Tools

- knitting tube and needle
- 2 alligator clips
- 1-pound weight (heavy clip, pliers, a stone, or anything else)
- chain-nose pliers
- flush cutter
- crimping tool for size 2 crimp beads

Materials

- Beadalon, Soft Flex, or Tigertail wire thread—3 yards
- seed bead mix—one tube (different colors, sizes, and shapes together look great)
- 2 bead cones
- 2 stones (8 mm)
- 2 silver balls (5 to 6 mm)
- 15 x 20 mm oval stone
- 2 crimp beads and covers—size 2

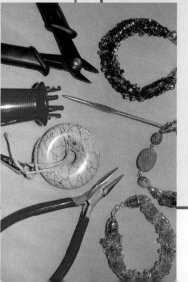

Here is the stone used as a weight for this project.

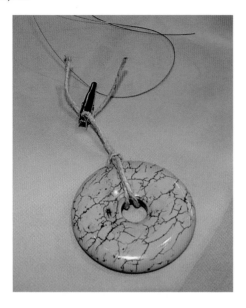

Tubes of assorted beads are great for this project.

Various manufacturers make knitting tubes. It's helpful to find a brand with notched pegs at the top or one that has a similar feature to help keep thread from slipping over the tops of the pegs.

When you remove the knitting tube from the package, you'll find the needle that accompanies it.

1. Attach an alligator clip near one end of the thread. The clip will keep the beads on the line while you assemble the piece. String beads onto about $1^1/2$ yards of the thread.

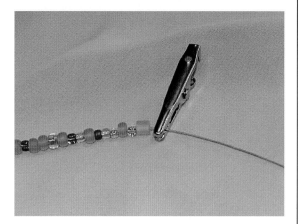

2. Feed the opposite end of the thread through the top center of the knitting tube.

3. With an alligator clip, attach the weight to the bottom of the thread you just fed through the tube. Your weight should dangle, not rest on the table, while you construct the necklace.

Try to keep the thread straight throughout the project to avoid kinks.

4. Begin to wrap the thread around a peg by starting it on the far side of your body, then wrap counterclockwise toward you, then over to the outside of the peg to the left of the first one, as shown.

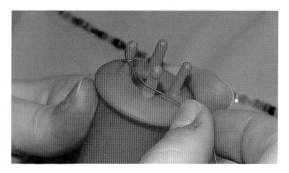

5. Wrap a loop around all four pegs this way: from the outside around to the inside, and back around to the outside of the next peg, moving counterclockwise around the pegs.

6. After wrapping the thread around all four pegs, pick up the needle and place it under the bottom strand of thread of one loop while placing your forefinger on the tip of that peg so as not to drop the stitch.

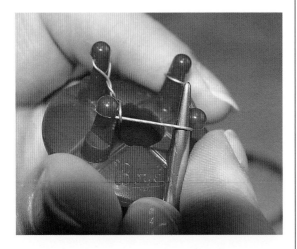

7. Lift this bottom thread over the top of the peg and remove the needle. One loop should remain on the peg.

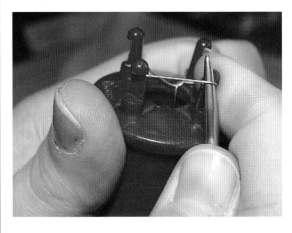

8. Repeat this process with the other three pegs.

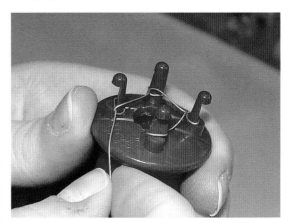

Continuously push the wrapped thread to the base of the tool with your fingers so the strands don't pop off the pegs.

9. Hold the thread down on each peg as you go. Although the loops want to pop off now, they become less stubborn as the knitting gets underway.

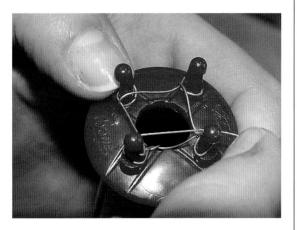

You want two loops on each peg so you can lift the bottom loop over the top one as you proceed.

10. Pull the strung beads up toward the top end of your line, close to where you've been weaving the thread, and refasten the clip to keep them in place.

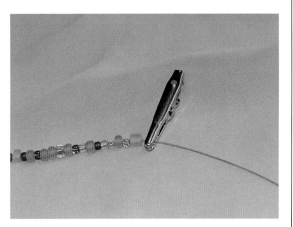

11. Bring up two or three beads to the top of the thread and let them fall so they lie on the thread between two pegs on the knitting tool. They will be "floating" on the thread between the two pegs. Wrap the wire around the peg to the right of the previous one, looping from the inside clockwise around the peg.

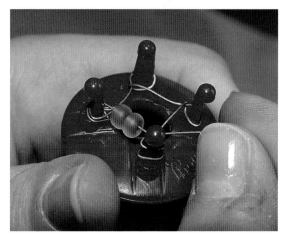

12. Lift the bottom loop over the peg that now holds a beaded thread.

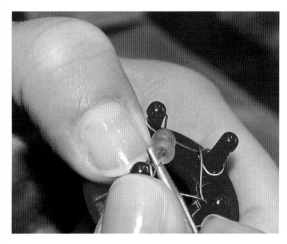

13. Make sure one loop remains on the peg.

Here's another view of the bottom thread about to be lifted over the peg.

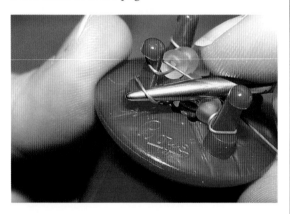

14. Add two or three beads (you decide—just be consistent) between each stitch.

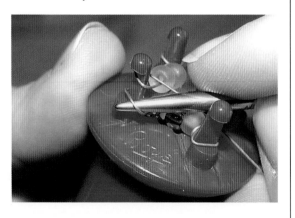

You can use larger beads if you skip a bead on the second one or two stitches to leave room for the beads to hang through the center of the knitting tube.

Remember to keep holding the thread at the base of the pegs with your fingers.

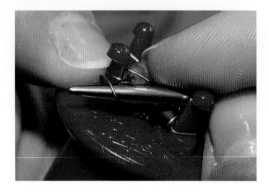

15. Continuously pull down on the center of the bracelet as it grows to help feed it through the center of the tube.

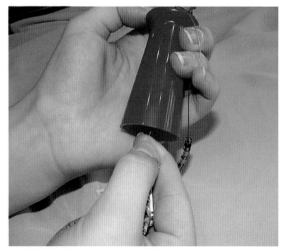

You'll know when you've slipped a stitch because there will be nothing left on the peg. You should have one line on each peg at all times.

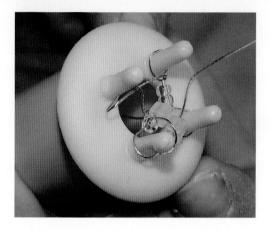

If you drop a stitch, pick up the thread with the needle and guide it with your finger to lift it back over the peg.

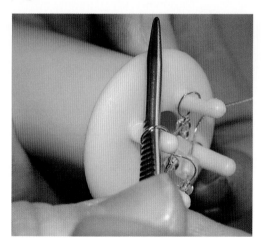

16. Continue your pattern: add two or three beads, loop the thread around the peg above the beads, pick up the bottom strand of the thread below the beads, and release a loop from the peg. Tug on the center to feed the beaded section through the center of the tube.

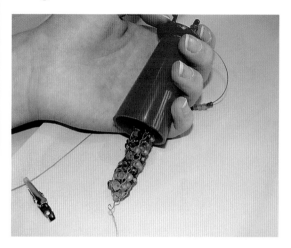

Here is how the bracelet looks after the knitting is complete.

Here is an example of a slipped stitch. To fix, take a piece of thread, string it through the loops, weave through the bracelet, then tie to secure. This will keep the whole bracelet from coming unraveled.

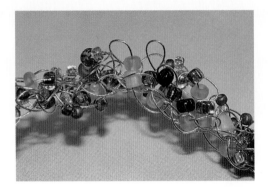

18. Gently remove the thread from the tool altogether. Use your needle if needed to loosen the thread from the pegs and lift the thread.

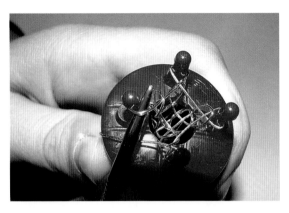

19. Loop the tip of the thread back through a nearby knitted section and pull tight to knot, sliding the knot down to the base of the knitted section. Repeat to be sure the knot is secure.

17. To finish, feed the end of the thread between the two strands of thread on each peg.

Here is a top view of how the thread will look after feeding it through.

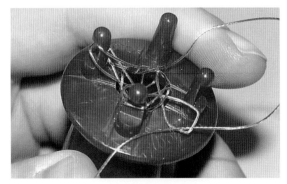

20. Remove the bracelet from the knitting tube and string a bead cone on the end so it covers the knot.

21. Next, string a small stone, a silver ball, a crimp bead, then the large stone.

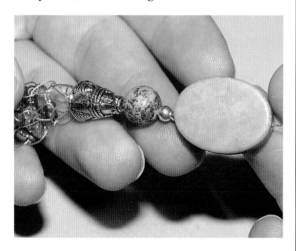

22. Complete a parallel sequence of stones on the other side of the large stone.

Modify this pattern as needed in order to fill the thread so the bracelet reaches a 7^1/$_2$-inch diameter.

23. Feed the thread through the large bead and the crimp bead on the opposite side of the bracelet. Then do the same with the thread on the opposite side, feeding it through the bead on the other side. You will have doubled-up thread through the beads on both sides when you're finished.

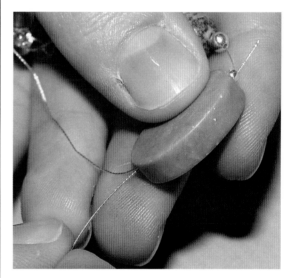

24. Tighten the thread to pull both ends of the bracelet together. Use a crimping tool to tighten the crimp beads, then attach the crimp covers.

25. Trim excess thread flush, but be very careful not to cut any other part of the thread.

26. Gently roll the bracelet onto your wrist. Because there is some give, you don't need a clasp for this one. Enjoy!

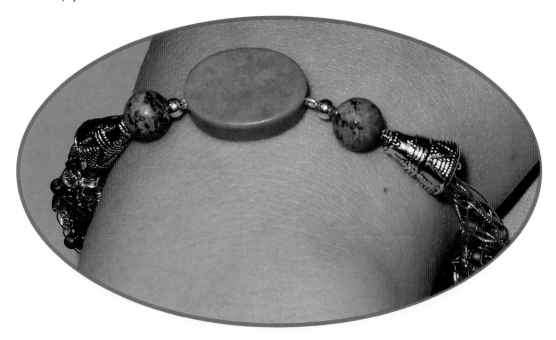

Part Two

Metal

Riveting and Cold Connections

Cold connections allow the artist to attach items without soldering, incorporating altered-art techniques. This technique requires no wire wrapping and only minimal beading if you choose. You can jump right in without experience here and just have fun piecing together your truly unique found objects.

Tools

- round-nose pliers
- chain-nose pliers
- flush cutter
- vise
- jeweler's file
- large shears (if needed to cut metal for base)
- ball-peen hammer
- Dremel drill, with collet nut small enough to fit a $^1/_{16}$-inch drill bit
- $^1/_{16}$-inch drill bit
- center punch
- wood block (to prevent you from drilling into your table)
- bench block
- #2 emery paper
- safety glasses/goggles

Materials

- found objects: scrap metal or copper plating (ask a silversmith or go to a junkyard or recycler), broken jewelry pieces, single old earrings, foreign coins, tackle, old goggle lenses, bottle caps, puzzle pieces, and so on
- metal beads for finishing
- 14-gauge wire
- 18-gauge wire—two 8-inch lengths
- chain, collar, ribbon, or leather cord to attach pendant
- 2 large Swarovski crystals

You'll need a $^1/16$-inch drill bit—exactly—so double check to ensure accuracy.

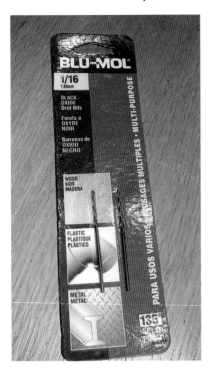

The $^1/16$-inch drill bit is almost the same diameter as the 14-gauge craft wire you'll be using in this project.

Here are some found objects that are ideal for this project. Perhaps you can conjure up a similar stash after a visit to your jewelry box or a second-hand store.

Narrow your stash of items down to those that caught your eye and experiment with creating a design out of some of the pieces.

1. Begin by choosing a piece of scrap metal or something flat to use as the base of your piece.

2. Cut the base down to the size you want.

Then file the corners so they aren't so sharp.

3. Choose the pieces you'd like to use on your base, and play with their arrangement until you find the way you want it to look. Now that you have a plan, you can continue with the assembly of the piece.

4. Cut a $1/2$-inch strip of 14-gauge wire with flush cutters, leaving a flat tip.

It's important to get a smooth, clean cut when making a rivet. The wire shown here was cut with the wrong side of the flush cutters—the tip is not flat.

Wrong

5. Clamp the wire vertically into a vise so about half is visible above the clamp.

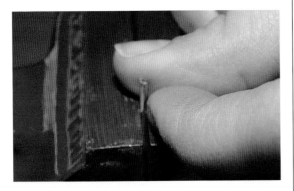

6. With a ball-peen hammer, hammer gently all around the outside of the tip of the wire, creating a mushroomlike head, similar to that of a nail.

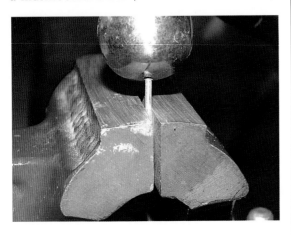

This is your first rivet.

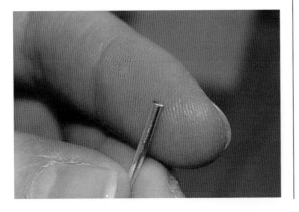

7. Tap the center punch once firmly with the ball-peen hammer, marking the spot on your piece where you want your first rivet to go.

8. Load the drill with the $^1/_{16}$-inch drill bit.

Be sure it is secure. Follow Dremel package instructions carefully to avoid injury. Wear safety goggles for this project.

9. It's a good idea to cover your hand with an oven mitt or hot pad (not shown) to hold the base firmly—metals can get hot from the drill. Check to be sure that the wood block is positioned under the base. Decide where you want to attach your first object and drill a hole through the base. Next drill a hole through your object. You'll feel when the drill has passed all the way through the pieces. The more dense the metal, the longer it will take to drill through it.

If you do not hold the pieces firmly while drilling, they could fly off the table with the force of the drill!

10. Put the rivet through the drilled holes in the base and the object, with the flattened tip (or head) on the back (or bottom) of the piece.

11. Use the flat side of a flush cutter to trim the wire, leaving a very small amount to hammer.

12. Place a bench block under the objects you will hammer to avoid driving the rivet into the wood. Hammer around the edge of the trimmed wire tip, just as you did to create the rivet, forming a lip like the head of a nail. This process will hold your pieces securely together.

If you're having trouble getting your pieces secured, flip the piece over and hammer the back side of the rivet again. It's very important that your wire gauge (14) and drill bit size ($^1/_{16}$) are right, or you may not be able to get your pieces to tighten upon riveting.

If your wire becomes bent while working with it, just straighten it out and continue.

On your next rivet, you might attach a bead for interest.

After your bead is affixed, hammer the rivet head flat to secure it.

13. Make another rivet with wire and attach it where you need it, repeating steps 4–12.

If the drilled hole gets too big, just put a bead or a bead cap on top of the wire before trimming and hammering to secure. This also helps if the surface of the piece you're riveting is raised or uneven.

This piece is getting a jolt of color.

A foreign coin adds interest as well.

Color, shape, texture—all work well together on this design.

14. Create a brushed finish on the copper or other metal base by rubbing the piece gently in one direction with emery paper. This step is optional, depending on your design.

Now let's do the finishing touches.

15. Center punch . . .

riveting and cold connections § **91**

16. . . . and drill a hole at the top of the piece. This is where you will attach wire to make the bail.

17. Make a loop with two strands of 18-gauge wire and thread it through the hole.

18. Tie off the wire, creating a knot. To do this, thread the two strands through the loop.

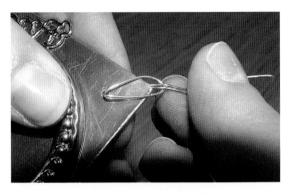

19. Add a Swarovski crystal onto the pair of long strands of wire.

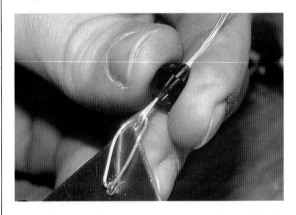

20. Create a small loop at the top of the wire, above the crystal, using round-nose pliers. Wrap the wire a few times just above the top of the crystal.

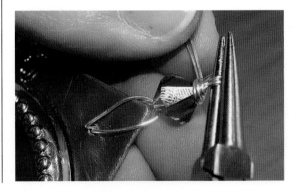

21. Use the flat side of the flush cutter to trim away any excess.

22. With chain-nose pliers, bend the loop to create the shape you desire.

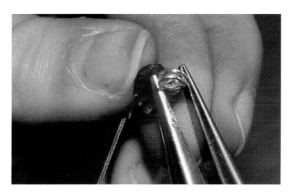

23. Use the chain-nose pliers to twist the visible wire into an interesting design.

24. Rub the back of the metal base with emery paper to be sure there are no rough edges. Rub in one direction to create a uniform brushed finish. It should be smooth against the skin or the fabric on which the piece will sit.

The finished piece is eclectic yet balanced and absolutely original.

Precious Metal Clay

recious Metal Clay, or PMC, begins as drab, pliable clay and ends as actual silver in your own unique design. The process takes you from rolling and stamping to dehydrating, firing, and burnishing. With a small investment in unusual items such as a small butane torch and a food dehydrator, you can create countless silver heirlooms. This might be the most impressive jewelry you've made yet!

Torches sell for $30 to $50. The less-expensive models may not have a childproof feature, and you may not be able to control the flame as well as you can with a slightly pricier model. If you are more expert than the rest of us, and you already have a kiln, use that instead!

It's a good idea to read through all the instructions before beginning, so you have an idea about the process. It helps to proceed deliberately, at least until the PMC is placed in the dehydrator, as it begins to dry out on its own.

Tools

- food dehydrator
- stamps
- playing cards
- small rolling pin (or a similar shape)
- emery board
- small sipping/stirring straws
- X-Acto knife, roller, scraper, paintbrush (buy as a set from Le Petit Artist)
- Badger Balm or olive oil
- tiny oval cookie cutter (for calla lillies only)
- plastic film page protector (available at office supply store)
- baby wipes
- agate or stainless steel burnisher
- small artist's paintbrush
- small bowl of water
- fireproof stone (to place under torch when firing)
- butane torch and butane
- polishing pad
- polishing cloth
- wire bristle brush
- silver blackener

Materials

- 16-gram package of PMC3 (clay)
- PMC3 syringes with clay, immersed in water
- 15 grams PMC3 paste (also called "slip" or "glue")
- 4 mm cubic zirconia ("CZ")
- chain or collar to attach pendant

- Note: If you don't have a food dehydrator, you can use a blow dryer and a cardboard box. Also, you don't have to use a cubic zirconia, but you want the stone you use to be able to withstand heat.

Before opening your package of PMC, have a rough idea of what you'll want to create. You'll want to work quickly because the clay will dry out.

If the slip dries up, add water to it. If it gets moldy, you can clean out the mold or just stir it up and it will be fine. If the clay dries up, you can grind it down and use that, too.

Since the water and binder in PMC3 vaporize when it is fired, PMC3 shrinkage rate is approximately 10 percent. When finished, your jewelry is 99.9 percent pure silver.

Pendant

1. Tape a sheet of plastic film page protector to your table. This will be your work surface.

2. Apply Badger Balm or olive oil to your fingers, fingertips, plastic work surface, and roller until they are lightly covered. This keeps the clay from sticking.

3. Open the PMC3 package, as well as the cellophane inner liner, and take out about half of the clay to use now. Rewrap the remaining clay in plastic wrap and close it to preserve it for later. Scrape off any extra clay from the cellophane. You want to use every bit because it is pricey.

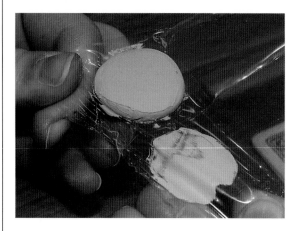

4. With the palms of your hands, roll the clay into a ball. If there is a crease in the ball, put that face-up on your work surface. The more you handle the clay, the quicker it dries.

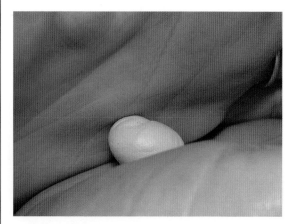

5. Make two stacks of four playing cards each. Place one stack to the left and one stack to the right of the clay to help you achieve the correct thickness when you roll it out.

6. Roll out the clay with the roller until it is the same thickness as the four-card stacks.

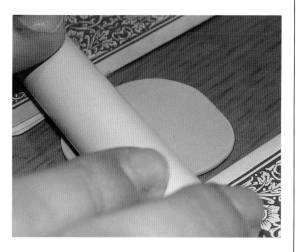

7. Remove one card from each stack so three cards remain on each.

8. Apply Badger Balm to the stamp pattern you will use.

9. Lift the clay with a scraper. Place the clay on top of the stamp pattern, then place the three-card stacks to the left and right of the clay. Roll over the clay to make an impression.

10. Remove the clay from the stamp with your fingers.

11. Rub a playing card with Badger Balm.

12. Place the clay pattern-side down on the card.

13. Pick up a stirring straw and rub it with Badger Balm.

14. Lay the stirring straw across the top of the clay, horizontally, and roll the top of the clay over the straw.

15. Dip the paintbrush into the slip.

16. Dab just beneath where the clay wraps over the straw. Use slip liberally—this, too, will turn to silver.

17. Dab the tip of the clay as well, then roll a bit more so the clay forms a closed loop. You're basically gluing the top of the piece into a bail, where a necklace chain will go through later.

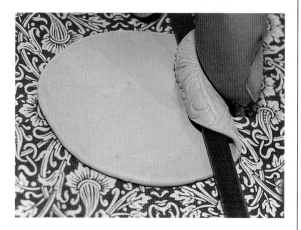

18. Flip the piece over so the patterned side faces up. Keep the straw in place until after step 26.

19. Test a syringe to be sure the clay inside it is soft enough to use without being watery.

20. Using another stirring straw, make a hole in the clay where you want your cubic zirconia to be placed. Do not make the hole too close to the edge.

The circle should pop out, sticking to the straw, like a cookie from a cookie cutter.

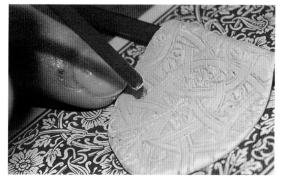

A cubic zirconia will be set in the hole.

21. Hold the syringe at an angle, rather than straight up and down, a bit above the hole. Carefully apply a ring of clay around the rim of the hole. Make a coil about one to three layers thick. The coil makes a bezel to hold the stone in place.

22. Place the stone into the hole, pointed side down. With the tip of the paintbrush handle, gently press the stone into the clay coil, making it level. Touch up the coil with slip if needed.

If you get extra clay on the stone, don't worry about it—you can gently scrape it off later.

23. You can stop here and create any additional pieces to layer on the base of your pendant. It's okay if this part of the clay dries. You can add to it later. Or, you can make smaller pieces, like flowers, ahead of time and attach them at this point.

Calla Lily Workshop

1. Place a small ball of clay between two stacks of two cards.

2. Roll out the clay to the same thickness as the two card stacks.

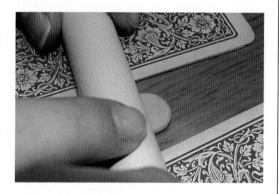

3. Coat your fingers with Badger Balm. With a tiny oval cookie cutter, cut out small pieces of clay to use for calla lily petals.

4. Lift the clay from the surface using the scraper.

5. Pinch the bottom between your thumb and forefinger to form the base of the lily. Put the flower on a card that has been rubbed with Badger Balm.

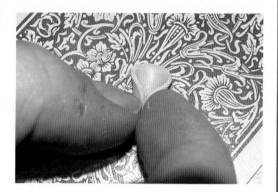

6. Add some slip to keep the piece together.

7. Roll out a tiny piece of clay with your fingers and trim off about a fingernail's length.

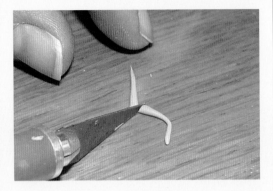

8. Place this small piece in the center of the oval.

9. Add some more slip to keep the pieces together.

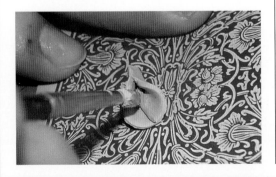

10. Put the pieces, card and all, into the dehydrator for 5 to 10 minutes, or until the clay lightens in color and hardens. (The state of the clay at this point is similar to the greenware state of pottery, if you're familiar with that process.)

Note: There's no danger of leaving the clay in the dehydrator too long, so don't worry about putting it back in if necessary.

11. Remove the lily from the dehydrator.

12. File the edges with an emery board as desired. It's best to do this before firing, because after firing, you'll have a strong metal that has to be filed with a jeweler's file, which is more work. It is easier to file clay than metal.

Note: You can make your own molds for these add-ons or buy them—this can help you make a variety of shapes and designs.

13. You can add slip where you want to build up the clay or smooth out a surface.

14. Affix the lilies to the base with slip. Choose an odd number of pieces—three works well—for a pleasing arrangement.

Border and Syringe Workshop

A strip of clay can be added as a border detail.

1. Roll out a small piece of clay one card thick.

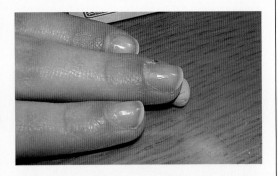

2. Use your hand to roll out the clay into a narrow worm or snake shape.

3. Use the roller to flatten it two cards thick.

4. Brush slip onto the base where the border will be affixed.

5. Affix the border, using as much or as little as you wish.

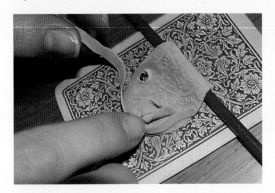

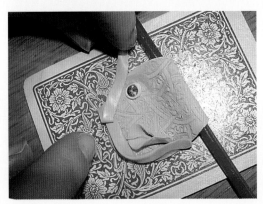

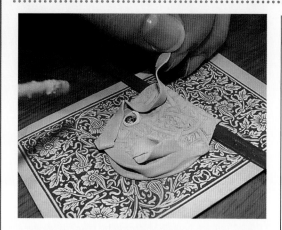

6. Now do some syringe work: add swirls for stems, a border, or any decorative touch. It's okay to improvise as you go—no need to overplan. If you don't like how your creative touches turn out the first time, just pull the border off and try again. When you're finished, cut the strip with an X-Acto knife.

24. Make additional holes now, near the bottom edge, if you'd like to attach beads after firing. (See Earrings section on page 113 to learn how.)

25. Put the entire piece into the dehydrator to dry.

26. After the clay has lightened in color (after about 5 to 10 minutes in the dehydrator), remove it and gently remove the straw from the top.

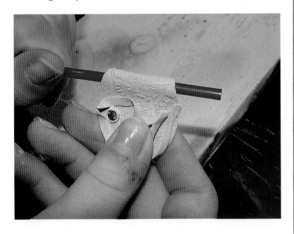

27. With the fine-grained side of an emery board, gently file around the outside edge of the piece, making a clean, even edge.

Tip: *Save your shavings to reuse in later projects.*

28. If there are any little dots or imperfections on the surface of the lilies or the piece, you can rub them with a baby wipe to achieve a smooth surface. Be careful to avoid rubbing any clay with a stamped design in it, though, as this will wipe out the pattern.

If necessary, use the X-Acto knife to carefully scrape away any excess clay covering the stone on the front of the piece. You may want to hold the stone in place while you do this, making sure you don't force it loose. When you hold the piece up to a light source, light should shine through the stone.

If your stone does pop out at this point, put it back in place, put more slip around it with a brush or syringe, and put the piece back into the dehydrator for a few minutes. Your piece must be totally dry before it is fired.

29. Follow the package instructions to install a butane cartridge into a butane torch. The torch should be childproof. Practice lighting it and setting it to ignite a continuous flame.

30. Place your pendant on a fireproof stone or soldering block. Place slate, charcoal, glass, or any other fireproof substance underneath the block to prevent the table getting too hot.

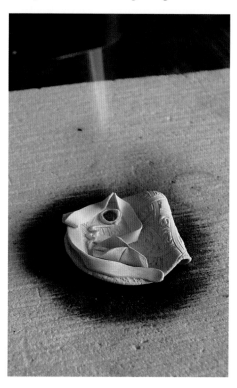

To avoid melting the clay, keep the torch 2 to 3 inches above the piece, using a circular motion, to ensure a brick-red color. If the piece glows cherry red, it is too hot and may melt. If this happens, remove the flame for a few seconds to let the piece cool down a little, then resume the firing process.

31. Be sure you are in a well-ventilated area; open windows or doors if you can. Start your torch on a continuous flame and swirl it about 2 to 3 inches above your pendant, moving evenly and continuously over the face of the piece, for about 5 minutes. Hold the flame straight over the piece—not at an angle. This will ensure an even distribution of heat.

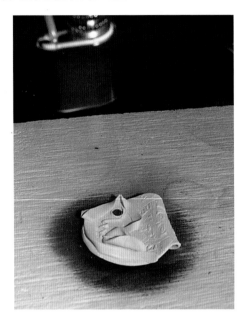

The PMC will turn *brick red* and could catch on fire. *Yes, catch on fire!* This is part of the process, so don't be alarmed. The edges of the piece may begin to curl a bit temporarily; the whole piece will then begin to shrink.

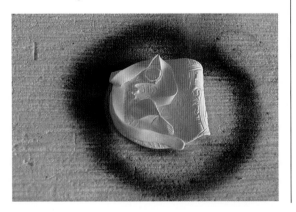

32. After you have fired the piece for 5 minutes, you are finished firing. Turn off the torch and give your shoulder a rest. *Do not touch the pendant at this point—it is very hot!* Let the stone cool down by itself. Do not submerge it in water—this will break the stone.

33. After the pendant cools, gently brush over it with a wire bristle brush, exposing the silver and making the piece shine. This is a magical step in the process—your clay is now metal.

34. Be careful to avoid brushing over the stone here, as it may scratch.

35. With an agate burnisher, polish all around the nooks and crannies of the piece until it is shiny. Don't worry too much about polishing the grooves in the piece.

36. You can use a smaller brush as well; this one rolls out like a pen and works well for smaller spaces. Burnishing tools typically come in sets, so you can play around with what works best for your piece.

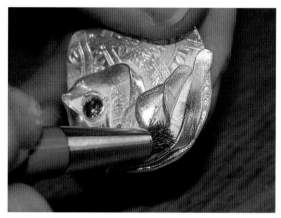

Try not to use any sharp tips of the burnishing tools, as they may leave noticeable scratches on the surface of the piece.

37. Put the pendant on a layer or two of paper towels. Dip a small paintbrush into the bottle of silver blackener, then brush it on the nooks and crannies and all of the piece.

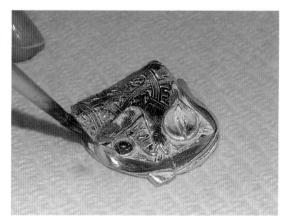

This piece is about as black as we want it to be.

38. Dip the piece in water to stop the blackening process. The blackener really brings out the pattern in the stamp you chose and gives it more depth.

- You don't need to brush the back of the piece with blackener.
- Do not leave your paintbrush in the blackener. It will eat away the bristles.
- You can also just dip the entire piece into a small bowl of blackener—this will make it darker.

39. Rub the higher surfaces with a polishing pad.

40. Then do the same with a polishing cloth.

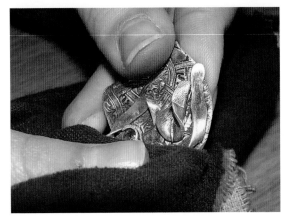

Your piece is now complete and ready to hang from a silver chain or collar. Now that you know the process, you are ready to experiment with your own creative ideas on future pieces. Enjoy!

Earrings

You can design earrings with a similar stamp pattern as your pendant to make a matching set, or simply choose shapes and dangles to capture a whimsical feel.

Materials

You'll need all the tools and materials listed at the beginning of the chapter, and also:

- 2 French hooks
- 16 beads to hang from the earrings
- 6 headpins
- 20-gauge wire—ten lengths of about 2 inches each
- chain-nose pliers
- flush cutter

1. Place a small ball of clay between two stacks of four cards each on your plastic film work surface.

2. Use the roller to flatten the clay into a circular or oblong shape.

3. Choose a stamp pattern to use on your earring.

4. After rubbing the stamp with Badger Balm, place the clay on the stamp.

5. Using three cards on either side, roll over the top of the clay on the stamp to make the impression.

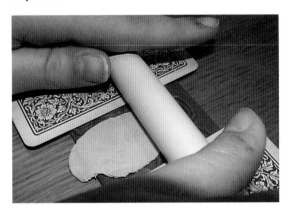

6. Remove the clay from the stamp and place it face up on a playing card that's been coated with Badger Balm.

7. Using an X-Acto knife, trim around the outside edge of the pattern to shape the piece as you desire.

8. Use a sipping straw to make a hole in the top of the earring; this is where the French hook will be attached.

9. If the "donut hole" didn't come out when you lifted the straw, lift it out with the tip of an X-Acto knife.

10. Make a few holes at the bottom of the piece as well, where you will hang beads later.

11. Follow steps 24–40 for the pendant project (pages 106–110)—the process is the same here.

12. Place the desired bead on a headpin, then make a loop at the top above the bead, using round-nose pliers.

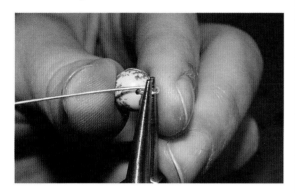

13. Hold the loop with chain-nose pliers, and wrap the wire twice with your thumb and fore-finger to secure the loop and the bead in place.

14. Trim the excess wire with a flush cutter.

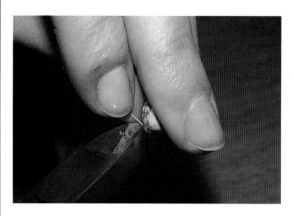

15. Pinch the trimmed edge with chain-nose pliers to avoid a sharp protrusion.

16. Make a loop at the tip of a short wire, leaving an opening wide enough to slip on the beaded loop.

17. Attach the bead to the wire loop.

18. Add another bead.

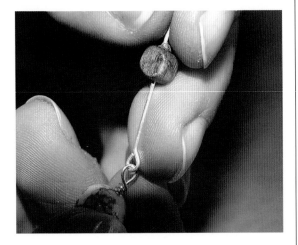

19. Thread the wire through one hole on the earring and make a loop.

20. Wrap the wire twice to anchor, trim off the excess wire with flush cutters, and pinch with chain-nose pliers to bend in the sharp end of the wire.

21. Repeat this process twice to add beaded dangles to the other two holes on the earring. You might make the middle dangle three beads long (instead of two) for variety.

22. Thread the last length of wire through the top hole of the earring.

23. Hold the looped wire with chain-nose pliers.

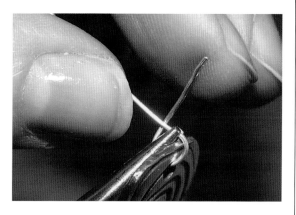

24. Use your thumb and forefinger to wrap the wire twice, securing the loop.

25. Trim away the excess wire and pinch the sharp edge in with chain-nose pliers.

26. String a bead onto the wire.

27. Now make a loop above the bead and trim the excess wire.

28. Twist open the loop of a French hook.

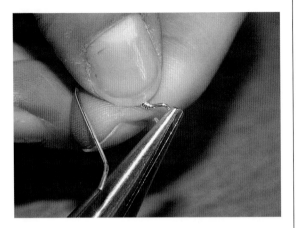

29. Slide the earring onto the hook's loop.

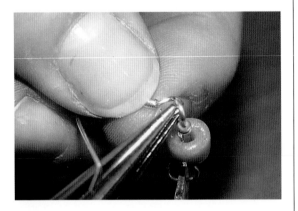

30. Twist the hook's loop shut again with chain-nose pliers.

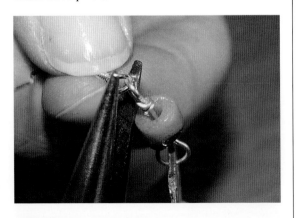

Your finished piece will be as unique as you are. (Don't forget to make a matching earring to complete the pair!)

Resources

Suppliers

Bey's Rock Shop
615 Route 100 North
Boyertown, PA 19512
610-369-0180
www.beysrockshop.com

House of Gems, Inc.
607 South Hill Street
Suite PL-02
Los Angeles, CA 90014
877-436-7123
www.houseofgems.com

Jewelry Supply (online only)
866-380-7464
www.jewelrysupply.com

Le Petit Artist
267 Carsonia Avenue
Mount Penn, PA 19606
610-779-9000
www.lepetitartist.com

Periodicals

Art Jewelry
21027 Crossroads Circle
Waukesha, WI 53187
800-533-6644
www.artjewelrymag.com

Bead Unique
P.O. Box 459
Mount Morris, IL 61054
800-935-3631
www.beaduniquemag.com

Beadwork
201 E. Fourth Street
Loveland, CO 80537
800-272-2193
www.interweave.com/bead/beadwork_magazine

Lapidary Journal Jewelry Artist Magazine
300 Chesterfield Parkway, Suite 100
Malvern, Pennsylvania 19355
610-232-5700

Simply Beads
P.O. Box 8000
Big Sandy, TX 75755
800-282-6643
www.simplybeadsmagazine.com

About the Consultant

....

Carolyn Yohn McManus, a native of Chester County, Pennsylvania, has been a master silversmith and goldsmith for over twenty-five years. She has a degree from the Bowman Technical School in Lancaster, Pennsylvania, and graduated from the Jewelry Design Institute in Richmond, Virginia. Carolyn also attended the Baum School of Art in Allentown, Pennsylvania, William Holland School of Lapidary Arts in Young Harris, Georgia, and has earned PMC level one and two certifications. She gained experience working as a bench jeweler for local fine jewelry stores. She has created a unique line of sterling silver multi-metals with semiprecious stone jewelry. She has been featured in the national magazine *Art Jewelry.*

Carolyn also designs and fabricates multi-metal sculptures. Her work has been accepted into many regional juried shows and fine art exhibits. She teaches classes in silversmithing, beading, wire wrapping, glass fusing, and PMC.

Also Available From Stackpole Books

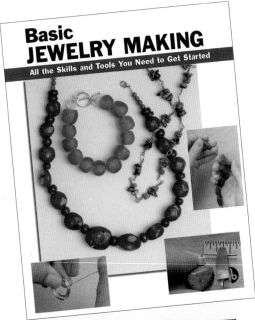

BASIC JEWELRY MAKING

$19.95, 128 pages, 490 color photos, 12 illustrations, 978-0-8117-3263-5

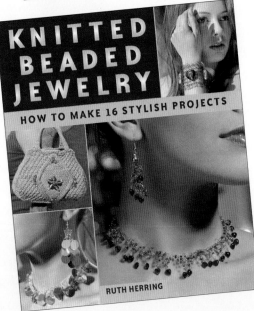

KNITTED BEADED JEWELRY

Ruth Herring

$16.95, 96 pages, 160 color photos, 8 illustrations, 978-0-8117-3501-8

Available at your favorite retailer, or from Stackpole Books at (800) 732-3669

STACKPOLE BOOKS

www.stackpolebooks.com